STEP INTO SUPERNATURAL POWER

Walking in the Spirit

NELLIE ODHUNO-SHANI

STEP INTO SUPERNATURAL POWER

Copyright © 2013 by **Nellie Odhuno-Shani**

All rights reserved.

Published by

Integrity
Publishers Inc.

P.O. Box 789,
Wake Forest, NC 27588
U.S.A.
info@integritypublishers.org
www. info@integritypublishers.org

ISBN: **978-1-937455-15-6**

Publishing Consultants:

PUBLISHING
Institute of Africa

P.O. Box 16458 – 00100
NAIROBI
KENYA
info@publishing-institute.org
www.publishing-institute.org

Reproduction, copy or transmission of this publication may not be made without written permission from the author or in accordance with the provisions of the Copyright Act of the United States of America.

Printed in the United States of America

Table of Contents

Dedication	v
Acknowledgement	vii
Introduction	ix
1 Who Is The Holy Spirit?	1
PART ONE: THE HOLY SPIRIT'S SUPERNATURAL POWER IN THE OLD TESTAMENT	5
2 Power For Innovation	9
3 Power For Leadership	13
4 Power For Battle	21
5 Power For Character	31
PART TWO: THE HOLY SPIRIT'S SUPERNATURAL POWER IN THE NEW TESTAMENT	39
6 The Holy Spirit And Jesus	41
7 Spirit Of Boldness	49
8 The In-Filling Of The Holy Spirit	51
9 The Gifts Of The Holy Spirit	61
10 Speaking In Tongues	101
Conclusion	113
About The Author	115

Dedication

Precious Holy Spirit, You have taught me so
much as I have written this book.
I totally dedicate this book to You!

Acknowledgements

Energized by the Holy Spirit, this book was written in record time. My first thanks go to Him who has become such a close Friend, Counsellor, Teacher and Companion. He opened my eyes to see truths that I have never before seen in the Word of God although I have been reading the Bible cover-to-cover since 1992!

God in his abundant mercy, and knowing that two are better than one, has given me a dear friend and prayer partner in Kitenge Shomba. May God bless you for standing with me and praying with me during the writing of this book. At times your prayers were so heartfelt and passionate one would have thought that you were the one writing the book! I would like to thank my editor, Irene Mumo. Your commitment and free service is not free in heaven. God bless you! I also would like to thank my publishers, Integrity Publisher, through Barine Kirimi. You have kept pushing me to keep publishing for the body of Christ. Thank you for your encouragement. I would also like to thank all the team members of Breaking Barriers International (BBI), David Odhuno, Dan Ole Shani (my beloved husband), Agiso Odhuno, Zenah Nyathama, Lydia Chola Waiyaki, Agnes Odero, Dr. Jane Awiti, Dr. Miriam Omolo, Sarah Oiro, Stella Nakitare, Carine Dheve, Isaiah Oiro, Eric Raymond Odhuno, Caroline Omolo, Elizabeth Odongo, Maureene Mushira, and Professor Adhiambo Odhuno – You have all been a great support!

Introduction

This is probably not the first book that you are reading about the Holy Spirit. The King James Version of the Bible calls Him the Holy Ghost. I believe that the precious Holy Spirit is one of the most misunderstood personalities in the Bible. Believers in Jesus Christ have "crossed swords" as they have argued over what His purpose in the Christian life really is. Some have called Him "It" or "Something" as they confess how "something" told them to do a certain thing. Others think that He is a nebulous power that manifests in believers when their emotions have been stirred. Tears are therefore often closely connected to the move of the Holy Spirit, in a lot of people's minds. A person will walk away from a meeting claiming "The Holy Spirit moved powerfully!" which translated, often means that there was a lot of show of emotions – crying, trembling, shouting, raising of hands, falling to the ground etc. – Nothing could be further from the truth, as we will see as we study the word of God!

While the majority of Christians will agree over His importance in leading people to a saving knowledge of Jesus Christ, even that is not "cast in stone." An altar call with soft music in the background while the preacher asks the non-believers where they would go, if as they were leaving the church building and a car hit them and took their lives on the spot, has often replaced the gentle wooing of this mysterious Being. As much as many of us believe that it is the Holy Spirit who convicts of sin (John 16:8), it is not uncommon to meet people who help Him in this task, by telling people how hot hell is! If that does not convince them, then they will be told to consider the possibility that that could be their last day on earth.

Although the Holy Spirit is present and busy in the whole Bible, most times He is relegated to the New Testament and more specifically, to the book of Acts after the Day of Pentecost. What was the Holy Spirit's role in the Old Testament? Was He looking on at all that was going on as He waited for the Day of Pentecost? How is He recognized in the life of a believer? Is His presence **in a believer** the same as His presence **upon a believer**?

Is "speaking in tongues" really necessary? What is the use of speaking to God in a language that we do not understand if we can speak to Him in a language that we understand? How does "speaking in tongues" benefit the people around me?

Unfortunately many churches have split up as a result of not being in full agreement concerning the manifestations of the Holy Spirit, and His working within the body of Christ. How sad that must make Him feel.

This is a book on spiritual warfare and as such it emphasizes the role of the Holy Spirit in this warfare, both in the Old Testament and in the New Testament. What was the Holy Spirit's role, in the warfare between David and Goliath; Samson and the Philistines; Gideon and the Midianites?

The best person to introduce the Holy Spirit is the Holy Spirit Himself! My prayer is that as you read this book, the Holy Spirit will reveal Himself to you in a way that has never happened before. He is wonderful! He is awesome! Without Him we cannot know Jesus or God the Father. He has been given full jurisdiction to move in and upon people on earth, to fulfil the will of the Father. As you continue reading this book may God stir up in you the Spirit of wisdom and revelation so you may know Him better (Ephesians 1:17).

1

Who Is The Holy Spirit?

OFTEN WHEN WE ARE ASKED TO INTRODUCE ourselves we start off by saying our name then immediately tell people, **what we do**. When somebody asks you, "Who are you?" it is different from "What do you do?" Unfortunately people often get their identity from what they do rather than from who they are in their "inner man". A new- born baby is important and has great value, long before they go to school and pursue a career.

The truth is that who we truly are is who leaves our body to go to heaven or hell when we die. Man is a spirit, has a soul, and lives in a body. What is truly important, what gives life to the body is the spirit. "As **the body without the spirit is dead**, so faith without deeds *is dead*" – James 2:26. Who your spirit is, is who you are. No more, no less! Our career and vocation is not that important at the graveyard. Whether people considered us beautiful, successful, highly educated or rich does not really count when an epitaph is being made to put on our grave. Usually our date of birth and our date of death is enough! When a person's spirit leaves their body that is the end of everything that mattered here on earth. It is interesting, how greatly human beings fear bodily harm. We fear sickness and disease, and go to great lengths to make sure that our homes are secure from thieves and robbers. After all they not only steal our physical property, but can also harm us physically! The Bible tells us whom we should really fear. "*I tell you, my friends,* **do not be afraid of those who kill the body and after that can do no more***. But I will show you whom you should fear: Fear him who after the killing of the body, has power to throw you into hell. Yes, I tell you, fear him*" – Luke 12:4-5.

In the same way, the Church of Christ is called the Body of Christ. "*And God placed everything under his feet and appointed him to be head over everything for* **the church, which is his body,** *the fullness of him who fills everything in everyway*" – Ephesians 1:23. If the Church is the Body of Christ, and the body without the spirit is dead, then it follows that **the Church without the Spirit is dead**! What is the remedy for a dead church? The remedy is the entrance of the Spirit because "**The Spirit gives life . . .**" – John 6:63. It should not come as a surprise that the birth of the Church of Jesus Christ was heralded by the coming of the Holy Spirit, in Acts chapter two. Three thousand people were added to their number that day! What could not be accomplished by the personal training of the disciples by Jesus Christ Himself for three years was accomplished in a day through the power of the Holy Spirit! The "church leaders" who had been hiding in a locked room for fear of the Jews on the day of Jesus' resurrection (John 20:19) were immediately transformed into bold and fearless evangelists, willing to be thrown into prison and also killed for the Gospel of Jesus!

No wonder Jesus warned them not to venture into ministry until they had received the gift of the Spirit. "...*He gave them **this command**: 'Do not leave Jerusalem, but wait for the gift my Father promised, which you have heard me speak about'*" – Acts 1:4. Waiting to receive the gift of the Holy Spirit was a command and not an option. Here was a group of people who had a very important task ahead of them. They were going to spread the Gospel to the rest of the world. They needed power to do this and Jesus gave them only one option – wait for the Holy Spirit! "*But **you will receive power when the Holy Spirit comes on you**; and you will be my witnesses in Jerusalem and in all Judea and Samaria, and to the ends of the earth*" – Acts 1:8. You and I constitute "...the ends of the earth." The Gospel has reached us because the disciples waited to receive power.

Who is this Holy Spirit who even Jesus needed to be baptised with before He started His earthly ministry? "...***God anointed Jesus of Nazareth with the Holy Spirit and with power**. And how he went around doing good and healing all who were under the power of the devil because God was with him*" – Acts 10:38. Jesus humbled Himself and let John baptise Him because He knew that to fulfil the will of His Father on earth, as a man, He needed the power of the Holy Spirit. As John baptised Him, the Spirit descended on Him like a dove. It was only after the Holy Spirit came upon Jesus that He was now ready to face the devil! "*Jesus, **full of the Holy Spirit**, returned from the Jordan (where John had just baptised Him) and was* *led by the Spirit into the desert, where for forty days he was tempted by the devil...*" – Luke 4:1-2.

It is interesting that while Jesus Christ was on the earth there were only two people who were filled with the Holy Spirit – Him (Jesus) and John the Baptist. Listen to what an angel told Zechariah, John's father, "*...For he will be great in the sight of God...and he will be filled with the Holy Spirit even from birth*" – Luke 1:15. John had to be filled with the Holy Spirit in order for him to fulfil the mission for which he was born. Can you and I need the Holy Spirit's power any less for us to fulfil the purpose for which we were born?

As Jesus approached His death, He told His disciples about the fact that the work that He had started while here on earth was going to be continued by the Holy Spirit. While Jesus was on earth, He was the Counsellor who revealed who the Father was and who told them what His will was. In John chapter sixteen He tells them of another Counsellor. "*And I will ask the Father and He will give you another Counsellor to be with you forever*" – John 14:16. Jesus told them that this Counsellor was not a stranger to them. "*...But you know him for he lives with you...*" – verse 17. What was Jesus saying? Did the disciples live with the Counsellor? – Absolutely! It is Jesus who lived with them and **He** was the Counsellor! Jesus went on to tell them that the Counsellor was coming to live **in** them. "*...And he will be in you*" – verse 17. Jesus could not live in the disciples in bodily form. He had to come in another form in order to live in them. That is why He told them "*I will not leave you as orphans; **I will come to you***" – verse 18. How was Jesus going to come to them? As the Holy Spirit – Praise the Lord! He assured them that they would continue to "see" Him because He was coming back to live in them as the Holy Spirit! "*Before long, the world will not see me anymore, **but you will see me***.

*Because I live, you will also live. On that day you will realise that I am in my Father, and you are in me and **I am in you**"* – Verse 19-20. How was Jesus going to be in them? - Through the Holy Spirit. Often when we say, "**I myself will be there**" we are simply emphasising the fact that it will not be someone representing me but that I will be there. This is exactly what Jesus said in John 17:26 at the end of His prayer for all believers. "*. . . In order that the love you have for me may be in them and that I **myself may be in them**.*" Jesus is saying that He Himself is in us as the Holy Spirit!

How were they going to see Him? He was going to show Himself to them through a love relationship with Him " *. . .He who loves me will be loved by my Father, and **I will love him and show myself to him**"* – verse 21. When we see the work of the Holy Spirit in the church, it is Jesus revealing Himself to us!

Everybody has a name that they respond to when they are called. Does the Holy Spirit have a name? "The Holy Spirit" is not His name any more than "The wife of Dan" is my name. The name that I go by is Nellie. He is the Holy Spirit, but does He go by any name? Actually the Holy Spirit has a name that He answers to! In John 14:26 we find out what that name is! "*But the Counsellor, the Holy Spirit whom **the Father will send in my name**, will teach you all things and will remind you of everything I have said to you.*" There it is! The Holy Spirit comes in the name of Jesus. That means that when you call on that name, it is the Holy Spirit that says, "Here I am!" – Praise the Lord! Not only does the name "Jesus" belong to the Holy Spirit it, also belongs to the Father. In John 17:11 we read " *. . .Holy Father, protect them by **the power of your name - the name you gave me** – so that they may be one as we are one.*" Jesus is saying that not only is He and the Father one, they share the same name! What name did God the Father give His Son? – JESUS. Jesus is telling God that God gave Him His (God the Father) name – JESUS. We see here how the Father, Son and Holy Spirit share the same name. When we call on Jesus, we are calling on all three personalities! The same reverence and awe that we give God the Father and the Son, is the same reverence that we should give the Holy Spirit! When a person is speaking in tongues, we are hearing the voice of the Father and the Son as well. He is not a wind, power or emotion. He is a person!

PART ONE

The Holy Spirit's Supernatural Power In the Old Testament

2

Power for Innovation

THERE ARE A LOT OF CHRISTIANS WHO BELIEVE that the Old Testament has no relevance for the Christian life today. They proclaim that the New Testament, which is the "new wine," nullified the Old Testament.

The Bible is one story, which starts in Genesis and ends in Revelation. We see God creating the world, and the Holy Spirit is present. *"In the beginning God created the heavens and the earth. Now the earth was formless and empty, darkness was over the surface of the deep, and the **Spirit of God** was hovering over the waters"* – Genesis 1:1-2. He creates Adam and Eve and places them in the Garden of Eden. Then we see them sinning and being chased from the Garden. They are separated from God as a consequence of their disobedience. Out of great love, God puts in place a plan for redeeming them through the blood of His son Jesus Christ. God chooses a tribe through whom His Son will come to the earth. We are shown the battles that this small tribe has to go through to preserve their lineage through which the Saviour of the world will come. Many prophets prophesy about the coming of God's Son. When the time is right, God sends a messenger angel to a virgin in Nazareth, a town in Galilee to tell her that she will give birth to the Son of God. Jesus is born and we are given an account of His ministry here on earth until He is crucified for the sins of the world. Jesus reconciles Man back to a loving relationship with His father through His death and resurrection. He trains His disciples to carry on the mission that He started, which is destroying the works of the devil. Jesus ascends into heaven. The Holy Spirit is sent to empower the church in their mission. His Church continues to witness, asking people to repent and be saved. We are told that He is coming again to take His Bride (the Church) to heaven.

It is impossible to see where to break this love story between God and His children, calling one part old and irrelevant. Throughout this story the Holy Spirit is very active, empowering, strengthening, encouraging, revealing, and giving wisdom! We see Him involved in physical battles as well as in spiritual battles. We see Him empowering ordinary men and giving them supernatural power thus enabling them to do things that they would not have been able to do in their natural power. We will look at a few of these men in the Old Testament and see how the Holy Spirit helped them in accomplishing the work that God gave them to do.

BEZALEL

The first time that we see the Holy Spirit at work after the creation of the earth is in Exodus chapter thirty- one. God had just given Moses the impossible task of building the Tabernacle where the presence of the Lord was going to reside. To understand how impossible this task looked, let us read just a portion of one of the tasks that God gave to Moses. *"Make curtains of goat hair for the tent over the tabernacle – eleven altogether. All eleven curtains are to be the same size – thirty cubits long and four cubits wide. Join five of the curtains together into one set and the other six into another set. Fold the sixth curtain double at the front of the tent. Make fifty loops at the end of the end curtain in one set and also along the edge of the end curtain in the other set. Then make fifty bronze clasps and put them in the loops to fasten the tent together as a unit. As for the additional length of the tent curtains, the half curtain that is left over is to hang down at the rear of the tabernacle"* – Exodus 26:7-12.

Can you imagine God giving you these directions and expecting you to follow them perfectly? I can just imagine a tailor being given these directions by a customer! This instruction was just a tiny portion of one of the eighteen things that God asked Moses to prepare for the Tabernacle! Was God expecting Moses to carry out these instructions on his own? Thankfully the answer is no.

God chose a man to oversee and carry out the work that God gave Moses. God did not choose a clever, hard-working man or intelligent man. We are not told that he had any skills when it came to craftsmanship. We are simply told *"See, I have chosen Bezalel son of Uri, the son of Hur, of the tribe of Judah"* – Exodus 31:2. The only thing that we know about Bezalel is that he was a descendant of a

God-fearing family. His "prayer warrior" grandfather, Hur, was the only Israelite who went with Moses and Aaron to pray at the top of a hill overlooking where Joshua was fighting the Amalekites. *"As long as Moses held up his hands, the Israelites were winning, but whenever he lowered his hands, the Amalekites were winning. When Moses' hands grew tired, they took a stone and put it under him and he sat on it. Aaron and Hur held his hands up – one on one side, and one on the other – so that his hands remained steady till sunset. So Joshua overcame the Amalekite army with the sword"* – Exodus 17:11-13.

The thing that qualified Bezalel was his godly heritage and not his natural ability. Interestingly, Bezalel's name means, "In the shadow of God". In Psalm 91:1 we read, *"He who dwells in the shelter of the Most High* **will rest under the shadow of the Almighty**.*"* The Psalmist goes on to say, *"He is my refuge and my fortress,* **my God in whom I trust**" – verse 2. Bezalel's trust in God also qualified him to be chosen. The final thing that caused Bezalel to be chosen by God was his willingness to serve. In Exodus 36:2 we read that Moses summoned " *...Every skilled person to whom the Lord had given ability* and **who was willing to come and do the work**."

Was his godly heritage enough for him to accomplish the work that God was giving him? - This mammoth task? We find the answer in the next verse. *"And I have filled him with the Spirit of God, with skill, ability, and knowledge in all kinds of crafts – and to make artistic designs for* **work in gold, silver and bronze, and to cut and set stones, to work in wood** *and to engage in all kinds of craftsmanship"* – verses 3-5. Wow! While a lot of people spend lots of money going to training seminars and workshops to learn skills, knowledge and ability for their various trades, believers in Christ need only to ask the Holy Spirit to endow them with a supernatural anointing. When

Moses is describing the people that God chose to do the work of the Tabernacle he says *"He has filled them with skill to do all kinds of work as craftsmen, designers, embroiderers in blue, purple and scarlet yarn and fine linen, and weavers – **all of them master craftsmen and designers**"* – Exodus 35:35.

The Holy Spirit is the Master artist! He gives supernatural abilities, skill, and knowledge! – Hallelujah! The Holy Spirit is a Master in all kinds of crafts; He makes artistic designs in gold, silver, and bronze; He also cuts and sets precious stones; He also works in wood! Are you involved in artistic crafts? Do you set stones? Are you a carpenter? To produce supernatural designs, be filled with the Spirit of God! Let the Holy Spirit give you ability, skill and knowledge. Christians should produce supernatural designs! They must be the ones who set the standards for excellent work. A dining room table made by a spirit-filled believer must be much more beautiful than that made by somebody using their natural ability? When we see an exceptionally cut gemstone we must be able to say, "That must have been cut by a Christian!" It is through spirit-filled believers that God shows the excellence of His kingdom! Whatever we do, we should do it as though as soon as we finish, an angel is going to take it to heaven to present before God!

Are there people who work under you in your business? God also chose and anointed all the people who were supposed to help Bazalel in the work of the Tabernacle. *"Moreover I have appointed Oholiab son of Ahisamach, of the tribe of Dan, to help him. Also I have given skill to all the craftsmen to make everything I have commanded you"* – verse 6. In the Bible we find that God puts a lot of emphasis on names and their meanings. He changed Abram's (meaning 'high father') name to Abraham (meaning father of many nations). The names often denoted the vocation of the individual. The meaning of Oholiab's name is very interesting since he was the one chosen to help Bezalel do the work in the Tabernacle. The Tabernacle was a tent. It is therefore very interesting to note that the name Oholiab, means "Father's tent"!

In Exodus 35:34 we find out that not only did God give Bezalel and Oholiab skill and ability for themselves, but He also gave them the divine ability to be able to pass on this skill to others. *"And He has given both him and Oholiab son of Ahisamach, of the tribe of Dan,* **the ability to teach others***."* When God commands us to do something, the Holy Spirit who resides in us equips us – Praise the Lord! All we need to do is ask for His help. How often have we struggled in our own strength to accomplish difficult tasks? *"If you then, though you are evil, know how to give good gifts to your children, how much more will your Father in heaven give the Holy Spirit to those who ask him!"* – Luke 11:13.

3

Power for Leadership

A LEADER IS A PERSON WHO HAS THE ABILITY to make others follow them willingly. They are pace setters. If you look behind you and no one is following you then you are not a true leader. Leaders have the ability to make others change **their** way of thinking to follow their way of thinking. It is no wonder that there are leaders who have lead thousands down the path of destruction. Adolf Hitler is one such example! Leadership, especially when we are called to lead a whole nation can be a fearful and intimidating thing.

SOLOMON

After King David died, his son Solomon took over the nation of Israel. While his father David fought battles all his adult life, Solomon inherited a very peaceful Kingdom. The Lord had said to King David, "*But you will have a man who will be a man of peace and rest, and I will give him rest from all his enemies on every side. His name will be Solomon and I will grant Israel peace and quiet during his reign*" – 1 Chronicles 22:9. Solomon's name means "Peace."

Is governing a peaceful nation all that is needed for good leadership? We are going to see that peace was not all that Solomon needed. First of all his own father King David, said of him, "*. . .My son Solomon is young and inexperienced . . .*" – 1 Chronicles 22:5. Age was not on his side, and neither was his experience. It was a good thing that there was peace because Solomon had not fought a single battle! David tried to advise his son Solomon as best as he could to prepare him for leadership. "*May the Lord give you discretion and understanding when he puts you in command over Israel, so that you may keep the law of the Lord your God. Then you will have success if you are careful to observe the decrees and laws that the Lord gave Moses for Israel. Be strong and courageous. Do not be afraid or discouraged... Then David ordered all the leaders of Israel to help his son Solomon*" – 1 Chronicles 22:12-17. In the King James Version, verse 12 says, ". . .Only the Lord give thee **wisdom and understanding** . . .*"

It is quite obvious that David was worried about his son Solomon. However, David prepared Solomon well by telling him the two things that he needed above everything else – Obeying the commandments of the Lord and, Wisdom and understanding! As soon as King Solomon took over we are told, "*Solomon showed *his love for the lord by walking according to the statutes of his father David . . ."* – 1 Kings 3:3. King Solomon has often been credited with asking the Lord for wisdom and understanding instead of great riches. I think that King David is the one who should be credited with instilling into his son, what he needed for good and successful leadership. Hence, when God came to Solomon and told him to ask for anything he wanted, he asked God for what his father David had told him that he needed!

I believe that one of the marks of a good leader is to know your weaknesses. Solomon did not have any over-estimated views about himself. Listen to his humble plea before the Lord. God had just told him, "Ask for whatever you want me to give you." His response was, *"Now, O Lord my God, you have made your servant king in place of my father David. But I am only a little child and do not know how to carry out my duties. Your servant is here among the people you have chosen, a great people, too numerous to count or number. So give your servant a discerning (understanding, according to King James Version) heart to govern your people and to distinguish between right and wrong, For who is able to govern this great people of yours?"* – 1 King 3:7-9. We are told that this request pleased the Lord! It always pleases the Lord when we request for His help instead of relying on our own strength.

God told Solomon that He would give him a wise and discerning heart. How was God going to do this? There is only one person who gives wisdom and understanding. God connected Solomon with that person – The Holy Spirit! *"The Spirit of the Lord will rest on him* – **the Spirit of wisdom and of understanding** . . ." – Isaiah 11:2. Even in the Old Testament, the Holy Spirit was on hand to give wisdom, and understanding, to anybody who asked. Solomon was the wisest king who ever stepped the face of the earth. He had supernatural wisdom. We are told that people came from all over the world to hear his wisdom. The Queen of Sheba came all the way from Ethiopia to hear the supernatural wisdom of Solomon! We are told that "...*She came to test him with hard questions...Solomon answered all her questions; nothing was too hard for the king to explain to her...She said to the king, 'The report I heard in my own country about your achievements and your wisdom is true. But I did not believe these things until I came and saw with my own eyes. Indeed not even half was told me; in wisdom and wealth you have far exceeded the report I heard"* – 1 Kings 10:1-7 Solomon's achievements and wisdom as a leader of Israel far exceeded what the Queen of Sheba had heard! Christian leaders' achievements and wisdom should far exceed anything that anybody has seen or heard. Where the Holy Spirit is, there is always the supernatural!

JOSHUA

One wish that Joshua must have had in the secret chambers of his heart must have been the Moses should live forever! That way he would never have to take over from him to lead the stubborn and obstinate people of Israel. Joshua had seen how quick they had been to turn to worshiping another god when he and Moses went up the mountain and came back after forty days. Moses had been a powerful leader who had led over a million people across the wilderness for forty years!

His leadership skills were greatly tested as the Israelites rejected him. After he sent out spies to go and look at that land, the report they brought back was so bad that the people said, "...*We should choose a leader and go back to Egypt*" – Numbers 14:4. As part of

Joshua's overall training in faith, he had also gone on this mission. Only Joshua and Caleb passed this test, of faith in God's promises. After this Moses' own brother and sister, Aaron and Miriam, defied his leadership. *"Has the Lord only spoken through Moses . . .Hasn't he also spoken through us?"* – Numbers 12: 2 Joshua also saw how some two hundred and fifty prominent community leaders who were also members of the council rose up against Moses. They accused him elevating himself. *" . . .Why then do you set yourself above the Lord's assembly"* – Numbers. 16:3. The Israelites were definitely not an easy community to lead! They missed the leeks and garlic in Egypt and demanded for God to improve their diet of eating only Manna day and night! Moses 'finally lost his cool' and struck a rock twice in anger, instead of speaking to it as God had told him to do. God told him that as a result of that disobedience he was not going to enter the Promised Land. Moses asked God to raise a leader to take over from him. *"May the Lord, the God of the spirits of all mankind, appoint a man over this community . . .So the Lord's people will not be like sheep without a shepherd"* – Numbers 27:16-17

Filling Moses' shoes was not going to be easy, whichever way one looked at it. We can only imagine Joshua's anxiety the day when Moses finally passed the 'baton' over to him! *"I am now a hundred and twenty years old and I am no loner able to lead you . . .Joshua also will cross over ahead of you, as the Lord said"* – Deuteronomy 31:2-3.

God told Moses who was going to take over from him, and how to start preparing him for leadership. *" . . .Take Joshua son of Nun, a **man in whom is the Spirit**, and **lay your hand on him**. Have him stand before Eleazar the priest and the entire assembly and commission him in their presence. Give him some of your authority so the whole Israelite community will obey him"* – Numbers 27:18-20. The most important thing to God when choosing Joshua was that the Spirit of God was in him. Secondly, he had to have the anointing for leadership. When Moses laid his hands on Joshua, he transferred his anointing for leadership onto him.

In his leadership role, God told Joshua, *"No one will be able to stand up against you all the days of your life. As I was with Moses, so I will be with you; I will never leave you nor forsake you"* – Joshua 1:5.

Strength and courage are two very important virtues for a leader to have and God told Joshua four times in Joshua chapter one to *"Be strong and courageous"* (verse 6, 7 9 and 18). However what gave Joshua the power to do supernatural things was the Holy Spirit. *"Now Joshua son of Nun was filled with the Spirit of wisdom because Moses had laid his hands on him"* – Deuteronomy 34:9

If Joshua received the power to be a leader by receiving the Spirit of wisdom through Moses laying his hands on him then it means that Moses also had the Spirit of wisdom and that is what gave him supernatural abilities. After this powerful impartation, Joshua told the Israelites, " . . .*the Lord will do amazing things among you"* – Joshua 3:5. Armed with the Spirit of wisdom, Joshua could now confidently lead the Israelites into the supernatural. They finally came to the edge of the Jordan River, which stood before them and the Promised Land, and Joshua's first supernatural miracle happened! *"Now the Jordan is at flood stage all during harvest. Yet as soon as the priests who carried the ark reached the Jordan and their feet touched the water's edge, the water from upstream stopped flowing. It piled up in a heap a great distance, . . .The priests who carried the ark of the covenant of the Lord stood firm on dry ground in the middle of the*

Jordan, while all Israel passed by until the whole nation had completed the crossing on dry ground" – Joshua 3:15-17.

The Holy Spirit of God empowered Joshua so that he was able to fill in the shoes of a mighty man of God. He went on to lead the community and do great exploits. He led the Israelites in a march around Jericho for seven days while blowing trumpets and giving a shout on the seventh round. The walls of Jericho crumbled without his army lifting a finger! That battle was won in a supernatural way.

Joshua went on to be the only man in history, to have commanded the earth to stop revolving and it stopped! He was fighting a battle and felt that there was not enough day- light left for them to fight and win the war. " '...*O sun, stand still over Gibeon, O moon, over the valley of Aijalon.' So the son stood still, and the moon stopped, till the nation avenged itself on its enemies"* – Joshua 10:12.

Are you a Christian leader? Remember what we said about who a leader is. It is anyone who is influencing people to move a particular direction. A mother is a leader in her home just as much as a senior executive is a leader in his or her establishment. To influence others, we first need to have been influenced ourselves. Do you desire to do supernatural things way beyond your natural abilities? Both King Solomon and Joshua have shown us how. The Spirit of wisdom is none other that the Holy Spirit Himself. Isaiah 11:2, while speaking about Jesus Christ said, *"The spirit of the Lord will rest on him –* **the Spirit of wisdom** *and of understanding..."* Both Solomon and Joshua had the Spirit of wisdom and it empowered them to do supernatural things. The same Holy Spirit is available to every leader. The result can only be the supernatural!

Every Believer has the Holy Spirit living in them, the same way that Joshua was a man who had the Spirit living *in* him. However Joshua still needed the Holy Spirit to come **upon** him through the laying on of Moses' hands. He was now equipped to go out and do supernatural exploits for God! The Holy Spirit who dwells in the Believer is empowered to do supernatural exploits when the Holy Spirit comes **upon** them with power! *"But you will receive power when the Holy Spirit comes **on you** . . ."* – Acts 1:8.

4

Power for Battle

THE OLD TESTAMENT IS RIFE WITH ACCOUNTS of the battles that the Israelites had to fight once they got into the Promised Land. One would have imagined that once God gave the Israelites the land, then they would just occupy it and live in it peacefully. Many Christians share this view that once a person becomes a born-again believer, that they can now live a peaceful life without any battles. Anyone who has been a Christian for any considerable amount of time will attest to the fact that the Christian life is warfare. God has assured us that in this warfare Christ has already won the battle! He has already "given" us the land.

God had promised the Israelites that He was taking them to

a land of milk and honey. They probably thought that as soon as they arrived on this land, they would immediately start to enjoy the milk and honey. What they did not know was that other people were occupying the land that was being given to them. When they reached the hill country of the Amorites God said to them, *"See the Lord your **God has given you the land**. Go up and take possession of it as the Lord, the God of your fathers told you. Do not be afraid; do not be discouraged"* – Deuteronomy 1: 21. God had given them the land, but it was still not in their possession. They had to go into battle to take (possess) what had already been given to them.

This is a good place to bring up a principle that many Christians struggle with – understanding that we still have to possess what God has already given to us. For example, Jesus has already healed us by His stripes and wounds (1 Peter 2:24). I now need to "possess" that health by fighting the good fight of faith (1 Timothy 6:12). The rest of this verse says to *"Take hold of the eternal life to which you were called . . ."* Taking hold of what God has already given us usually requires a fight – a fight that we have already won. For example if I tell full-grown man that I have given them a ball but there is a two-year old boy that is holding their ball. Then I tell the man to go and fight the two-year old and get his ball. As the man approaches the two-year old boy, it is a battle that he has already won!

So God told the Israelites to take what was already theirs by fighting battles with the occupants of the land. We will now look at a few of these battles to see what part the Holy Spirit played in the victory that ensued.

GIDEON

Gideon lived at a very sad time in the history of Israel. After the death of Joshua the Israelites followed God for a little while then forsook Him. We are told, *"After that whole generation had been gathered to their fathers, another generation grew up, who knew neither the Lord nor what he had done for Israel"* – Judges 2:10. Apparently there was a generation that did not tell the next generation about God and what He had done for Israel. This is why God had told the Israelites in Deuteronomy chapter six, *"These are the commands . . .the Lord your God commanded me to teach you . . .so that your children and their children after them may fear the Lord your God as long as you live . . .Impress them on your children. Talk about them when you sit at home and when you walk along the road, when you lie down and when you get up. Tie them as symbols on your hands and bind them on your foreheads. Write them on the doorframes of your houses and on your gates"* – Deuteronomy 6:1-9. It is very easy to see how children and grandchildren of a great man or woman of God can totally turn away from God because the "mantle" for the faith was never passed down to them by their parents.

The Israelites had done evil in the sight of God, and for seven years He gave them into the hands of the Midianites (Judges 6:1). Whenever the Israelites planted their crops, the Midianites would camp on the land and ruin their crops. To hide from the Midianites, the Israelites prepared shelters for themselves in mountain clefts, caves and strongholds.

When we first meet Gideon, he was threshing wheat in a winepress to keep it from the Midianites. He was demoralized and fearful. When an angel came and greeted him as a mighty warrior and telling him that the Lord was with him, he sneered, *"If the Lord is with us, why has all this happened to us? Where are all the wonders our fathers told us about . . . But **now the Lord has abandoned us** and put us into the hand of the Midian?"* – Judges 6:13. I believe that Gideon must have laughed when the angel told him that God was sending him to save Israel from Midian's hand. Gideon knew that he was not a warrior and that even if someone were to come and choose a man to lead Israel's army against Midian he would be the least likely.

Gideon's insecurity came from his perception of his background and lineage. *"How can I save Israel? My clan is the weakest in Manasseh, and I am the least in my family"* – Judges 6:15. If I were God, I would have side stepped Gideon and looked for a man with a little more self- confidence. Turning this man into a warrior seemed as likely as changing a caterpillar into a monkey! God ignored Gideon's mournful complaints and told him, *"I will be with you, and you will strike down all the Midianites together"* – Judges 6: 16.

Once God had convinced Gideon to be His warrior, He took away the first thing that stood in Gideon's way and that would have impeded him in his quest for victory. **"Tear down your father's altar to Baal** *and cut down the Asherah pole beside it"* – Judges 6:25. Gideon's family worshipped an idol and God could not have a warrior who was involved in idolatry. God had warned the Israelites that if they worshipped other gods, they would not be able to stand before their enemies (Leviticus 26:37). Was Gideon now ready for battle? Did he now have the courage and boldness to lead Israel against their enemies the Midianites?

We are told, *"Now all the Midianites, Amalekites and other eastern peoples joined forces and crossed over the Jordan and camped in the valley of Jezreel"* – Judges 6:33. The defining moment had come. Here was tiny Israel standing against all these nations to engage them in battle. Then God did the only thing that He knew was the deciding factor between strength and weakness; fear and boldness; defeat and victory! – He sent forth the Holy Spirit! *"**Then the Spirit of the Lord came upon Gideon**, and he blew a trumpet, summoning the Abiezrites to follow him. He sent messengers throughout Manasseh, calling them to arms, and also into Asher, Zebulun and Naphtali, so that they too went up to meet them"* – Judges 6:34. The Holy Spirit gave Gideon supernatural boldness and courage and turned him from a frightened young man into a fearless warrior for the Lord!

SAMSON

Just like Gideon's rise happened during a time when Israel had forsaken their God, Samson was also born at a time of great desolation. *"Again the Israelites did evil in the eyes of the Lord, so the Lord delivered them into the hands of the Philistines for forty years"* – Judges 13:1. During this time of hopelessness, "hope" was born to sterile woman by God's miracle. This child was Samson. Concerning this miracle baby an angel had told his mother, *"...You will conceive and give birth to a son. No razor may be used on his head, because the boy is to be a Nazirite, **set apart to God from birth**, and he will begin the deliverance of Israel from the hands of the Philistines"* – Judges 13:5.

Once Samson had been identified as the one who God was going to use in the battle against the Philistines, the Holy Spirit started His work of preparation. *"**And the Spirit of the Lord began to stir him** while he was in Mahaneh"* – Judges 13:25. Since the Holy Spirit was going to work a lot with Samson in his life, I think that the

Holy Spirit began to introduce Himself to Samson through these stirrings!

Many people who grew up going to Sunday school probably heard about the story of Samson. It is interesting that when children are asked to draw Samson, they often draw him as tall and huge with big bulging muscles on his arms and legs! Yet nowhere in the Bible are we told that Samson was a big muscular man! The reason why I think that Samson was probably a small man is because the Philistines kept trying to find out the source of his strength. They knew that it was definitely not in his physique. We are going to find out where the strength of Samson came from. Those that think that his strength came from his long hair are wrong! His hair had nothing to do with his strength. His hair had to do with the covenant that he had with God. What was the covenant? *"**No razor may be used on his head, because the boy is a Nazirite**, set apart to God from birth"* – Judges 13:5. The reason why Samson's hair was not supposed to be cut was not because of physical strength but because he was a Nazirite.

Samson was not the first Nazirite in the Bible. The first time that we hear about Nazirites is in the book of Numbers. Here God told Moses, *" . . .If a man or woman wants to make a special vow, a vow of separation to the Lord as a Nazirite . . .During the entire time of his separation no razor may be used on his head. He must be holy until the period of his separation to the Lord is over; he must let the hair of his head grow long. . .because the symbol of his separation to God is on his head. Throughout the period of his separation he is consecrated to the Lord"* – Judges 6:1-8. Apparently God said nothing here connecting a Nazirite to physical strength! So what gave Samson physical strength for his battles?

One time Samson and his parents were going to Timnath because he had seen a Philistine woman and he wanted her for his wife. As they were approaching the vineyards of Timnath and he was walking a distance from his parents, a young lion suddenly came roaring toward him! Did Samson have supernatural physical strength to tackle this lion? If Samson had relied on his natural physical strength, then we would never have heard about Samson again after this incident. What happened next is what saved his life! *"The Spirit of the Lord came upon him in power..."* – Judges 14:6. Once the Spirit of the Lord was upon him, he could do supernatural things. What did he do to the young lion? The rest of verse six says, " *...He tore the lion apart with his bare hands as he might have torn a young goat..."* It was the Holy Spirit who empowered Samson in his battle against the lion.

The next time we see Samson's supernatural strength was when the Philistine took his wife and gave her to another man. He got so angry that he burnt up their grain (Judges 15:1-5). After doing this he went and hid in a cave. The Philistines demanded that the Israelites hand over Samson to them so they could kill him. When the Israelites told Samson that they were going to hand him over to the Philistines, he complied after the Israelites swore to him that they would not kill him themselves. The Israelites tied him up with two new ropes and led him from the rock where he had been hiding, to hand him over to the Philistines. As Samson approached the Philistines, they came toward him shouting! Was this the end of Samson? Would his natural strength help him escape? The Holy Spirit stepped in again! *"The Spirit of the Lord came upon him in power. The ropes on his arms became like charred flax, and the bindings dropped from his hands. Finding a fresh jawbone of a donkey, he grabbed it and struck down a thousand men"* – Judges 15:14-15.

Because Samson was a 'thorn in the flesh' to the Philistines, they continued to look for a way to subdue him. Their opportunity cam when Samson fell in love with a Philistine woman called Delilah. They told her, *"See if you can lure him into showing you the secret of his great strength and how we can overpower him so we may tie him up and subdue him"* – Judges 16:5.

After much badgering, Samson finally told Delilah what his parents must have told him. *"No razor has ever been used on my head, . . .because I have been a Nazirite set apart to God since birth.* **If my head were shaved, my strength would leave me.** *And I would become as weak as any other man"* – Judges 16:17. What Samson did not understand was that it was the Holy Spirit that would come upon him to give him because he was set apart.

Samson's story has a very sad ending. After Delilah cut his hair, she called the Philistines to come and capture him. Samson was asleep when the Philistines arrived. He woke up from sleep and thought, *" 'I'll go out as before and shake myself free.'* **But he did not know that the Lord had left him**" – Judges 16:20. Samson did not know that it was the Lord who came as the Holy Spirit who gave him strength because of the covenant that he had with Him as a Nazirite. It was not his hair that gave him strength. The Lord left him because they were not longer bound by the covenant. Once the Lord left him, he became like any other man. *"The Philistines seized him, gouged out his eyes and took him down to Gaze, Binding him with bronze shackles, they set him to grinding in the prison"* – Judges 16: 21-22. Samson lost his supernatural power when the Holy Spirit stopped coming upon him in power. Thankfully Samson's hair did grow again while he was in prison and the covenant was established once more. *"But the hair on his head began to grow again after it had been shaved"* – Judges 16:22. The Holy Spirit moved upon him one last time when he asked God to help him. " . . .*O Sovereign Lord, remember me. O God please strengthen me just once more, and let me with one blow get revenge on the Philistines for my two eyes"* – Judges 16:28. The Holy Spirit came upon Samson again and he was able to push the two pillars that were holding up the temple killing three thousand men and women!

This is the same Holy Spirit that Jesus talked about in Acts 1:8 when He said *"But you will receive power when the Holy Spirit is come upon you; and you will be my witnesses . . ."* The same power that released the supernatural in the Old Testament wants to do the same today!

5

Power for Character

AT A TIME WHEN ISRAEL WAS UNFAITHFUL TO GOD, He raised a prophet among them called Samuel. He was born from a barren woman, Hannah, who asked the Lord for him so that she could give him back to God. *"Samuel continued as judge over Israel all the days of his life"* – 1 Samuel 7:15. When Samuel grew too old to Judge he appointed his two sons, Joel and Abijah, to take over from him. However, these men did not have good characters. *"But his sons did not walk in his ways. They turned aside after dishonest gain and accepted bribes and perverted justice"* – 1 Samuel 8:3. This situation caused the elders of Israel to go to Samuel and seek a solution. *"So all the elders of Israel gathered together and came to Samuel at Ramah.*

They said to him, 'You are old, and your sons do not walk in your ways; now appoint a king to lead us, such as all the other nations have" – 1 Samuel 8:4. Basically what the elders were telling Samuel was that his sons had bad characters and so were unfit to judge. Although this request displeased Samuel (God had been their King up to this point), the Lord told him to give them a king as they had requested.

SAUL

The very first time that Samuel met Saul God said to him, *"This is the man I spoke to you about; he will govern my people"* – 1 Samuel 9:17. Up to this point the only thing that the Bible reveals about Saul is that he was an impressive young man without equal among the Israelites. We are also told something about his physical appearance – a head taller than any of the others (1 Samuel 9:2).

Concerning his character, we know that he was a humble man because when Samuel told him that God had chosen him, he replied that he could not have been worthy to lead Israel because he was from the smallest tribe in Israel (a Benjamite) and that his clan was the least of all the clans of Benjamin. Samuel was not to be deterred. He knew that this was God's chosen man, so when the time came, he anointed Saul. *"Then Samuel took a flask of oil and poured it on Saul's head and kissed him, saying, 'Has not the Lord anointed you leader over his inheritance?"* – 1 Samuel 10:1. With the anointing oil on him was Saul now ready to be God's kind of leader? - Apparently not. In verse 6 of the same chapter, Samuel tells Saul, **"The Spirit of the Lord will come upon you in power . . .and you will be changed into a different person."** Saul's character was going to be changed once the Holy Spirit came upon him with power – power to change his whole being! When Samuel presented Saul to the people he said, *"Do you see the man the Lord has chosen? There is no one like among all the people"* – 1 Samuel 10:24. Why was there no one like him? Was it because he was more special than anybody else in Israel? There was no one like Saul among the people because God had changed him into a different man when the Holy Spirit came upon him in power!

As long as Saul walked with God in total obedience, the Holy Spirit guided him. But when he started to rely on his own understanding, he turned away from God. *"I am grieved that I have made Saul king, because he has turned away from me and **has not carried out my instruction**"* – 1 Samuel 15:11. Even if the Holy Spirit comes upon a person, they still have to walk in obedience to God. It is a choice, which each person has to make. Once a person chooses to obey God, then the Holy Spirit helps them do the thing that God is asking them to do. As soon as Saul stopped walking with God his character changed and he became rebellious and arrogant (1 Samuel 15:23). Whereas the Holy Spirit was guiding him before, he now had an evil spirit that tormented him! *"Now the Spirit of the Lord had departed from Saul, and an evil spirit from the Lord tormented him"* – 1Samuel 17:27. With the departure of the Holy Spirit came a change of character.

The first negative character trait that we see in Saul is great anger and intense jealousy and fear! David had just killed Goliath, a Philistine who for forty days had taunted Israel and caused great terror in their camp. After the death of Goliath the women came out from all the towns of Israel, singing and rejoicing. It was a great day for Israel but not for Saul! Instead of rejoicing, all he remembered was that the women had sang that David killed tens of thousands while he had only killed thousands! *"Saul was very angry . . .and from that time* **Saul kept a jealous eye on David**" – 1 Samuel 18:8-9. David had risked his life for the nation but Saul did not appreciate it. On two occasions Saul hurled a spear at David in fierce anger, intending to pin him to the wall. On the second occasion we are told that he hurled the spear with such force that he drove it into the wall. An evil spirit had taken over his character and was the one now controlling him! Saul's character without the Spirit went from bad to worse and he eventually completely turned away from God and consulted a witchdoctor!

Samuel grieved deeply when God rejected Saul. After he rebelled and disobeyed God's command to kill the Amalekites, and not to leave animal or person alive; but instead he spared the king plus some fat animals; Samuel never made contact will Saul again until he died (1 Samuel 15:35).

Meanwhile Israel needed a leader with a good character and God set out to find the man so that Samuel could anoint. *"How long will you mourn for Saul, since I have rejected him as king over Israel? Fill your horn with oil and be on your way; I am sending you to Jesse of Bethlehem. I have chosen one of his sons to be king"* – 1 Samuel 16:1.

It is interesting how experience always influences us. Samuel's experience with how God had chosen Saul influenced, how he perceived the next king. He remembered how God had chosen an impressive young man who was a head taller than everybody else. As soon as Samuel had laid eyes on Saul, God immediately told him that he was the man that He had chosen to lead Israel. He was probably thinking that God would do the same thing again, and let him know immediately, which of Jesse's sons He had chosen. Although God knew who He had chosen, he let Samuel go through examining all seven sons, each time telling him that that was not the one He had chosen.

ELIAB

The first son that Samuel saw was Eliab. He must have been very impressive and tall like Saul and Samuel thought that his search was over! *"Surely the Lord's anointed stands here before the Lord"* – 1 Samuel 16:6. Here was an opportunity for God to teach Samuel something about how He chooses. Samuel had thought that God had chosen Saul because he was a head taller that everybody else. However, nowhere in the Bible does God say that He chose Saul because he was tall. God chose Saul, who happened to be tall. God read Samuel's mind and told him, *"Do not consider his appearance or his height,* **for I have rejected him.** *The Lord does not look at the things man looks at. Man looks at the outward appearance, but God looks at the heart"* – 1 Samuel 16:7.

It is interesting to note that when the other six brothers of Eliab passed before Samuel the Lord kept telling him, *"The Lord has not chosen this one either"* – 1 Samuel 16:8. God kept saying that He had not chosen them. However, with Eliab God did not say that He had not chosen him, but that **He had rejected him**! God told Samuel that He looks at the heart. When He looked at Eliab's heart, He rejected him. Eliab's name means "God is my Father." Despite God being his father, there was something wrong in his heart. He was angry, harsh, unreasonable, and a bad judge of character. The same way that many Christians, though calling God their Father, can still have serious character flaws!

The first time that we meet Eliab is when he and his two younger brothers went to join the Israelite army that Goliath was terrorising. David, the youngest of Jesse's sons, and who was a shepherd, had been sent by his father to take provisions for his brothers who had gone to war. When David arrived he heard Goliath insulting the God of Israel and turned to one of the men. *"What will be done for the man who kills this Philistine and removes this disgrace from Israel? Who is this uncircumcised Philistine that he should defy the armies of the Living God?"* – 1 Samuel 17:26. As the men were responding to David, Eliab his eldest brother was within earshot. He lashed out at David who had come to bring them provisions and was asking a very valid question.

Eliab's first reaction at seeing his brother was anger. " . . .*He burned with anger at him and asked, 'Why have you come down here? And with whom did you leave those few sheep in the desert? . . .' "* – 1 Samuel 17:28. There was nothing that David had done to cause anyone to burn with anger. If anything this was the first time that anybody was speaking hopefully about the situation. Eliab went on to remind David that he was a shepherd and had no business where warriors were!

In the same verse Eliab attacks David's character. *"I know how conceited you are and **how wicked your heart is**; you came down only to watch the battle."* This was Eliab's brother, yet he really did not know him. He judged David's heart - which only God can do - calling it wicked. He called David conceited yet we know that God opposes the proud, but still said that David was a man after His own heart! Eliab's vicious attack on David did not deter him. David's brother had just insulted him yet he simply ignored it. *"He then turned away to someone else and brought up the same matter and the men answered him as before"* -1 Samuel 17:29. Now we see why God not only did not choose Eliab, He rejected him although his name was "God is my Father." Eliab may have been the one who said that David should not be called to meet Samuel because with whom would he leave the few sheep in the desert? Although God did not choose Eliab's six brother, He did not reject them!

DAVID

Samuel must have wondered whether he had come to the right Jesse. After all he may not have been the only Jesse in Israel. God told him to come and anoint one of Jesse's sons as king yet God had not chosen any of them! He must have been puzzled as he asked, *"Are these all the sons you have?"* – 1Samuel 16:11. Oh there was one, but he was not that important. He was just a Shepherd. For Jesse not to call David to the meeting betrayed how he viewed David. Guess who may have influenced the way David was viewed by his family members – Eliab! Later on in verse 11, " *'There is still the youngest' Jesse answered, 'but he is tending the sheep.'* "

When David arrived, Samuel stood up and anointed him *"Rise and anoint him; he is the one . . .So Samuel took the horn of oil and anointed him in the presence of his brothers . . ."* - verse 13. Basically what God was saying, is "His heart is right!" Was the anointing enough? Was David now ready to be king? Was a right heart all that he needed? God was going to require David to not just have a right heart, but a supernatural heart! We usually marvel at how graciously David treated Saul who hunted him down to kill him. When Saul entered a cave where David and his men had been hiding from him, David spared his life. What is it that gave David that exceptional character? We see it at the end of verse 13. " . . . ***And from that day*** *on the Spirit of the Lord came upon David in power."*

When we follow the story of David in the Bible, what stands out are not the wars that he led Israel in, but his character! After he committed adultery with Bathsheba, he was very quick to repent and turn to God. While behaviour can be modified to suit a certain situation, our character - that inner person - can only be molded and influenced by the Holy Spirit!

PART TWO

The Holy Spirit's Supernatural Power In the New Testament

6

The Holy Spirit and Jesus

JESUS' STORY BEGINS IN THE OLD TESTAMENT and ends in the New Testament like a seamless 'garment.' Let me reiterate what I said in chapter two. The Bible is one story that starts in Genesis and ends in Revelation. Jesus tried to say this to His disciples while He was on earth. He told them that Moses talked about Him! When he joined the two people that were going to Emmaus after his death and resurrection we are told, *"And beginning with Moses and all the prophets, he explained to them what was said in all the*

Scriptures concerning himself" – Luke 24:27. Then appearing to his Disciples later on He told them that the Old Testament talked about Him. *"This is what I told you while I was with you: Everything must be fulfilled that is written about me in the Law of Moses, the Prophets and the Psalms"* – Luke 24:44

We therefore find that the Holy Spirit's coming to rest on Jesus was prophesied by the prophet Isaiah. *"A shoot will come up from the stump of Jesse; from his roots a Branch will bear fruit.* **The Spirit of the Lord will rest on him** – *the Spirit of wisdom and of understanding, the Spirit of counsel and of power, the Spirit of knowledge and of the fear of the Lord"* – Isaiah 11:2. The distinctive feature of the Holy Spirit when it came to Jesus was that He would **rest on Him**. In the Old Testament the Holy Spirit came to empower people to be able to do certain things and then He departed.

John the Baptist was the first person to attribute this resting of the Spirit on Jesus, after His baptism in the Jordan River. *"I saw the Spirit come down from heaven as a dove and* **remain on him***. I would not have known him except that the one who sent me to baptize with water told me, 'The man on whom you see the Spirit come down and remain is he who will baptize with the Holy Spirit'* **I have seen and testify that this is the Son of God**' *"* – John 1:32-33. John proved that Isaiah was speaking about the Holy Spirit coming to rest on Jesus.

After John baptized Jesus we are told that He was full of the Holy Spirit. This also shows us that the "Spirit" that Isaiah is talking about is the Holy Spirit that we see in the New Testament. *"Jesus, full of the Holy Spirit, returned from the Jordan and was* **led by the Spirit** *in the Desert"* – Luke 4:1. From this point on, the Spirit was in total control of everything that Jesus did. The first thing that the Spirit did was to lead Jesus in the desert to face the tempter. We need to be full of the Spirit no less than Jesus did, in order to be able to face the Tempter. It is the Holy Spirit that empowered Jesus to go without eating or drinking for forty days.

In Luke 4:14 we are told that Jesus returned to Galilee **in the power of the Spirit**. " . . . *And news about him spread through the whole countryside. He taught in their synagogues and everyone praised him.*" I believe that it is no coincidence that people now got to hear about Jesus. Jesus' ministry was launched out by the power of the Holy Spirit. The first place that Jesus read when He went to the synagogue and picked up the scroll was, the passage in Isaiah 61:1 "***The Spirit of the Lord*** *is on me, because he has anointed me to preach good news to the poor. He has sent me to proclaim freedom for the prisoners and recovery of sight for the blind, to release the oppressed, to proclaim the year of the Lord's favour*" – Luke 4:18. Jesus could not start His ministry on earth until the Holy Spirit had come upon Him in power! One of the things that became empowered was Jesus' teaching. The people were able to tell the difference between Holy Spirit inspire teaching, and dull legalistic teaching that they were used to. "*The people were amazed at his teaching, because he taught them as one who had authority and not as the teachers of the law . . .they asked each other, 'What is this? A new teaching – and with authority! He even gives orders to evil sprits and they obey him*" – Mark 1:22-27. Where the Holy Spirit is at work, people will always be amazed! They will look at what they are seeing and compare it to what they have always seen and will testify to the supernatural! Jesus Himself testified to where His power came from when He said, "***The Spirit of the Lord is on Me because He has anointed Me . . .***" We can desire no less if we want to do the things that Jesus did. He has told us that

45

anyone who has faith in Him (Believer) will do what He did. He has said that they will do even greater things than He did! – John 14:12.

Is it really possible to do greater things than Jesus did? Jesus would not have said that we would do even greater things than Him if He knew that it was impossible. To do what Jesus did, we should move under the same power that Jesus moved in. Jesus was anointed by His Father to do the things that He did, beginning in Galilee after He was baptised by John and spread out throughout Judea. His secret? *"How God anointed Jesus of Nazareth* **with the Holy Spirit and power,** *and how he went around doing good and healing all who were under the power of the devil because God was with him"* – Acts 10:38. Whatever Jesus did was by the power of the Holy Spirit!

JESUS' COMMAND

The time for Jesus' departure to go back to His Father was fast approaching. Jesus had been very focused during the time of His earthly ministry. He kept His goal ahead of Him. He even told His disciples that His food was to do the will of His Father who sent Him, and to finish His work. Jesus was totally consumed with finishing the work that His Father had sent Him to do. The greatest accomplishment for Jesus on the cross was that He had finally finished the work that His Father had given Him to do. With His very last breath Jesus said, "It is finished."

The end of Jesus work was, however, the beginning of work for His disciples. There was a Gospel to be spread beginning in Jerusalem, then Judea, then Samaria, and to the ends of the earth! One would have thought that the sooner that they started this gigantic mission the better it would have been for the spread of the Gospel. What kind of people was Jesus relying on? These were the disciples, most of whom had run away leaving Jesus all alone when the soldiers came for Him at the olive grove where they were. *"Then everyone deserted him and fled"* – Mark 14:50. We are told that a young man, wearing nothing but a linen garment, was following Jesus. When they seized him, he fled naked, leaving his garment behind! – Mark 14:51. Peter who had showed bravery by chopping off the ear of the servant of the High Priest later denied three times that he knew Jesus! Are these the kind of people that Jesus was relying on to carry the Gospel to the ends of the earth?

The disciples found each other again after they had scattered. It was now the third day since Jesus had been crucified. In the evening they met together, "…**With the doors locked for fear of the Jews**…" – John 20:19. Jesus came and stood among them. He did something very interesting to these shivering and scared disciples. *"Jesus said 'Peace be with you! As the Father has sent me, I am sending you' And with that* **he breathed on them and said, 'Receive the Holy Spirit**" – John 20:21-22.

This was the first time that the disciples were receiving the Holy Spirit. How was this 'Receiving the Holy Spirit' different from how the Holy Spirit would come upon them on the Day of Pentecost? I believe that this is the moment when they received the Spirit to **indwell them**, the same way that a Believer in Jesus Christ receives the Holy Spirit when they accept Him into their hearts as Lord and Saviour. He comes to indwell them. *"Because you are sons,* **God sent the Spirit of His Son into our hearts,** *the Spirit who calls out 'Abba, Father'"* – Galatians 4:6.

Apparently the indwelling Spirit come as a seal of ownership, to show that the person has become a child of God. He did not come to empower for supernatural ministry. Jesus knew that His disciples were not ready to go out and conquer the world for Him. That is why He gave them a command. "...***Do not leave Jerusalem, but wait for the gift my Father promised,*** *which you have heard me speak about... In a few days you will be baptized with the Holy Spirit*" – Acts 1:4-5. Who is this gift that the Father promised and who Jesus talked to His disciples about? The passage is found in John 14:16. "*And I will ask the Father and he will give you another Counsellor to be with you forever – the Spirit of Truth.*" The Spirit that Jesus commanded His disciples to wait for in Jerusalem was also called the 'Counsellor.' Why did they need to wait for Him? What role was this Counsellor going to play in their mission to evangelize the world? "*But you will receive power when the Holy Spirit comes on you; and you will be my witnesses in Jerusalem, and in all Judea and Samaria, and to the ends of the earth*" – Acts 1:8. The Holy Spirit had already come in them when Jesus breathed on them. Now He was going to come on them. Only this time He was going to come to impart power to be witnesses!

Jesus made it clear through this command that He gave to His disciples that is impossible for a person to be a powerful witness without the Holy Spirit coming upon them! If the disciples who had walked with Jesus everyday for three years needed this power, how much more you and I?

7

Spirit of Boldness

OUT OF ALL OF JESUS DISCIPLES, the one that seemed the boldest was Peter. He was one of the three disciples that Jesus took with him on missions where no other disciple was invited. Peter stood out from the rest for being the most vocal. When Jesus asked His disciples who they said He was, it was Peter's response that is recorded. " *'But what about you?'* he asked. *'Who do you say I am?'* **Peter answered**, *'You are the Christ'* " – Mark 8:29. Peter was also the one who resisted having his feet washed by the Lord, while the rest of the disciples seemed to go along with the idea. *"He came to Simon Peter, who said to him, 'Lord, are you going to wash my feet?'.. .'No.' said Peter, 'You shall never wash my feet'* " – John 13:6-8.

Unfortunately Peter's boldness came from believing that he knew better than everyone else, including Jesus! Peter, in his misplaced boldness was going to put a stop to this "madness." Why couldn't his colleagues see that it was not right for their Master to wash their dirty feet! Peter must have felt that this was the height of disrespect! That Jesus would do such a thing was shocking to Peter. He had to correct Jesus! Even after Jesus said to him that he did not realize what Jesus was doing, but later on he would understand, he still said, *"No. You shall never (not now, and not any other time!) wash my feet!"* Basically what Peter's problem was, was that if he allowed Jesus to wash his feet then he would also be expected to wash the feet of people that were "lower" than him and that he could not do! Peter was protecting his own dignity. To put it bluntly, Peter was a proud man! The rest of the disciples were humble enough to accept that Jesus was the Master and He could do whatever He pleased. Once Peter found out that it was "honourable" to have his feet washed, and that it would give him a part with the great Jesus, then he wanted it all! *"Then Lord...Not just my feet but my hands and my head as well"* – John 13:9.

One time Jesus was teaching His disciples and He told them that it was His mission on earth to suffer many things and be rejected by the elders, chief priests and teachers of the law, and that He must be killed and after three days rise again. This was again too much for Peter! He did not sacrifice his life to follow a loser! Peter probably thought that Jesus was just physically tired and was succumbing to having a "pity party." Jesus who was all powerful (healing sick people, rebuking demons and waves) was going to lallow Himself be killed by the elders, chief priests and teachers of the law? And the rest of the disciples are just quiet? Was Jesus in His right mind?

Peter figured that if he did not do something quickly, the whole group would go astray. He couldn't believe that the other disciples were saying nothing! Peter decided to be bold and help Jesus out! However, he was not going to embarrass Jesus publicly. He would speak to him privately. Perhaps Jesus would consider his idea and correct His way of thinking. " . . .*And Peter took him aside and began to rebuke him*" – Mark 8:32.

Rebuke is a very strong word. The dictionary says that it means to express **sharp disapproval or criticism** of (someone) because of their behavior or actions. This was the extent of Peter's misplaced boldness! He was "Mr. Right" and everybody else including Jesus were "Mr. Wrong"! Although Peter rebuked Jesus in private, Jesus responded to him in the hearing of all the disciples. "But *when Jesus turned and looked at his disciples he rebuked Peter*" – Mark 8:33. Jesus wanted all His disciples to learn that Satan did not influence us to have in mind the things of God, but the things of men (pertaining to the earth). Jesus was quick to see that Satan had already taken advantage of the fact that Peter was wise in his own eyes, to try and use him to derail Jesus. "***Do not be wise in your own eyes***; *fear the Lord and shun evil*" – Proverbs 3:7. Jesus knew that His battle was not against flesh and blood, and he wanted his disciples to also learn this lesson. It is for this reason that He said, "*Get behind me Satan!*" It was Satan who was using bold Peter.

Peter grossly overestimated his boldness. Who he perceived himself to be and who he really was, were like two parallel roads! When Jesus told His disciples that they were all going to desert Him on the night of His betrayal, Peter thought, "Jesus must not really know me!" Peter boldly said, "*Even if all fall away on account of you, I never will*" – Matthew 26:33. After Peter said this, Jesus said, "***I tell*** *you the truth, . . .*" – verse 34. What Jesus was telling Peter, was that he had believed a lie about who he really was. " . . .*This very night, before the rooster crows, you will disown me three times* (verse 34)." Even after Jesus told Peter the truth, he still felt that Jesus did not know the truth about him. "*But Peter declared, 'Even if I have to die with you, I will never disown you*" – verse 35. Peter was saying, "Jesus You are wrong!" Nobody knows us better than Jesus and Peter was going to learn that the bitter way.

We observe Peter's last show of boldness when Judas arrives with soldiers to arrest Jesus. When the men stepped forward and arrested Jesus, Peter flew into action! "*Then one of those standing near drew his sword and struck the servant of the high priest, cutting off his ear*" – Mark: 47. Peter's act of boldness was not acknowledged, as Jesus told him to put away his sword, and healed the man's bleeding ear. Then Peter's true nature began to show.

FEARFUL PETER

He had boldly declared that he was willing to die with Jesus, yet after Jesus was arrested and was being led to the high priest we are told "*Peter followed him **at a distance**, right into the courtyard of the high priest. There he sat with the guards and warmed himself at the fire*" – Mark 14:54. Peter distanced himself from Jesus the moment that He was led away. His Lord was facing the most agonizing time of his life, and Peter sat by the fire, warming himself and hoping that nobody would notice that he was one of Jesus disciples. Peter was not lucky that night.

While Peter was below in the courtyard, one of the servant girls of the high priest came by. She looked around, and saw Peter warming himself. *"You also were with that Nazarene, Jesus . . .But he denied it. 'I don't know or understand what you are talking about' "* – Mark 14:66-68. Peter stood up and went into the entryway to escape from the girl, but she saw him a second time and again told him that he was a disciple of Jesus and he denied it again. Then those standing near Peter said to him, *"Surely you are one of them, for you are a Galilean."* He probably had tried to strike up a conversation with them and his accent gave him away! This third time, the ugliness that was in Peter, spilt over. Ugliness, which three years with Jesus, had not been able to erase. *"He began to call down curses on himself and he swore to them, 'I don't know **this man** you're talking about"* – Mark 14:71. When push came to shove, Peter who had boldly declared that he would die with Jesus now called him "This man."

Jesus had told Peter that before the rooster crowed, he would deny Him three times. When the rooster crowed, Peter finally saw himself for who he truly was! The bitter tears that he shed were as a result of his "eyes" being open to see himself for the coward that he was, and not the bold man that he had made people think he was.

One can only imagine how Peter felt after denying Jesus. Peter and Jesus needed time alone so that their relationship could be restored. It is recorded that Jesus appeared to Peter alone after His resurrection. *" . . .It is true! The Lord has appeared to Simon"* – Luke 24:34.

THE SPIRIT COMES ON PETER

Peter was no longer confident in himself. After Jesus ascended into heaven, the disciples went back to Jerusalem and met constantly in an upper room where they prayed. No mention is made of Peter and his declarations again. Peter was there when the Holy Spirit came on the Day of Pentecost and fell on all of them. Jesus had told them that they would receive power when the Holy Spirit came upon them.

The first change we notice in Peter after he is filled with the Holy Spirit is boldness! This was the man who had denied ever knowing Jesus, and was with the disciples behind locked doors because they feared the Jews. Yet after the Day of Pentecost, Peter boldly stood before a large crowd of people from " . . .*Every nation under heaven*" (Acts 2:5), and preached to them about Jesus. "*Then Peter stood up with the Eleven, raised his voice and addressed the crowd . . .*" – Acts 2:14. Peter now had supernatural boldness to witness. He was no longer afraid of the Jews. "*This man was handed over to you by God's set purpose and foreknowledge;* **and you with the help of wicked men, put him to death by nailing him on a cross** . . .*Repent and be baptized every one of you, in the name of Jesus Christ for the forgiveness of your sins. And you will receive the gift of the Holy Spirit*" – Acts 2:23. What a transformation! This is a completely new and bold Peter, empowered by the Holy Spirit!

The next time we see Peter, he is with John going to the temple. They meet a man who was crippled from birth. When this beggar asks them for money, Peter looks straight at him with great boldness and says, "*Silver or gold I do not have, but what I have I give you. In the name of Jesus Christ of Nazareth, walk*" – Acts 3:6. After that Peter took the man by the hand and helped him up and the man began to walk! What power! What boldness! Only this time he does not put his confidence in himself but in the power of the Holy Spirit. Peter finally understood that what he now offered the world was not his own power, but the name of Jesus!

Peter is no longer afraid of the rulers, elders and the teachers of the law. Peter and John preached publicly and the number of the men who believed because of the miracle they had just done grew to about five thousand! Because of this they were thrown into prison and the next day appeared before the Jewish leaders and the high priest. They demanded, *"By what power or what name did you do this?"* – Acts 4:7. Peter no longer relied on his own understanding. We are told, *"Then Peter, filled with the Holy Spirit, said to them . . ."* – Acts 4:8. The Bible is careful to tell us that it was the Holy Spirit who gave Peter boldness.

The fear of witnessing is very common among Christians. In my first book, *Stand Your Ground: Perishing For Lack Of Knowledge*, I share my testimony about how difficult I found it to be bold and stand out as a Christian in university. The *Navigators* who I fellowshipped with required that we go door-to-door witnessing on campus on Saturdays and I would start sweating two days before! I relied on my own natural ability and did not have much success.

God has never intended that we go out and share about Jesus through our own boldness. Our total reliance must be on the ability and boldness that the Holy Spirit bestows on us as He comes upon us. The disciples of Jesus could not witness by their own power and neither can we. In a later chapter we will talk about how the Holy Spirit comes upon Believers.

8

The In-Filling of The Holy Spirit

THE IMMINENT DEPARTURE OF JESUS CHRIST to go back to His Father must have brought the disciples a lot of anxiety. His crucifixion and death had just exposed the fact that they were not yet ready to face the world and be faithful witnesses for Jesus. They had just failed the test of standing by Jesus in His hour of need. Now He was saying that He was going to the Father. Jesus sensed this turmoil when He told them, *"Do not let your hearts be troubled. Trust in God; trust also in me...I will come back and take you to be with me that you also may be where I am"* – John 14:3. How were they to survive the hostility of the Jewish leaders meanwhile?

The good news was that Jesus was promising to send someone who would be with them in His absence. *"And I will ask the Father, and he will give you another Counsellor to be with you forever – the Spirit of truth..."* – John 14:16-17. Other than telling them what the Spirit would do when He came (John 16:13-15), Jesus did not describe to His disciples, in what form He was going to come. Since He was "another Counsellor", was He going to come the same way Jesus came? Would He be born as a human being? I am sure the disciples thought the Holy Spirit was going to be sent, talking and walking on two feet like Jesus. He was going to guide them and speak to them.

THE DAY OF PENTECOST

As the disciples of Jesus were together probably praying and praising, suddenly a sound like the blowing of a violent wind came from heaven and filled the place where they were sitting. Let us assume that nothing else happened that day. Would they have thought that that wind was the Holy Spirit? I don't think so. Why? Because Jesus had told them *"But when the Spirit of truth comes he will guide you into all truth. He will not speak on his own; he will speak only what he hears, and he will tell you what is yet to come"* – John 16:12-13. The Holy Spirit was going to guide them into all the truth by **speaking to them** what He heard the Father saying and also tell them about the future. Did this violent wind qualify? How was this wind going to guide them and speak to them? A violent wind from heaven did not qualify as the Holy Spirit that Jesus was going to send.

After that they saw tongues of fire coming into the room, which separated and rested on each of them. These tongues of fire did not discriminate. They rested on each person. What if nothing else happened after that? Would the tongues of fire have guided them and taught them? I think not. Since Jesus had said that the Holy Spirit could speak, His arrival was going to involve the mouth!

The last thing that happened was *"All of them were filled with the Holy Spirit **and began to speak** . . ."* –Acts 2:4. The Holy Spirit was sent to speak to show that He had arrived. Speaking was going to be the sign that He had come upon a person. The only problem was that nobody could understand what the other person was saying. They did not even know that they were speaking. They just thought that each person was making a difference kind of sound. *"If then I do not grasp the meaning of what someone is saying, I am a foreigner to the speaker, and he is a foreigner to me"* – 1 Corinthians 14:11. The sounds that these disciples were making were so loud that the people outside the building heard it and came. They happened to be people from other nations who had come to Jerusalem on pilgrimage and " *. . .Each one heard them speaking in his own language. Utterly amazed, they asked: 'Are not all these men Galileans? Then how is it that each of us hears them in his own native language? . . ."* – Acts 2:6-8. The testimony of these foreigners is what convinced the disciples that the Holy Spirit had come and was speaking! What was He saying? *" . . .We hear them declaring the wonders of God in our own tongues!"* – Acts 2:11. This was totally supernatural. Therefore a manifestation of the Holy Spirit is the presence of the supernatural. When the Holy sprit comes upon a person, one will not be left wondering whether the Spirit had come or not. It is a supernatural experience, and does not leave people the same way that He found them – Praise the Lord! Speaking in tongues, then, is a sign that the Holy Spirit has descended!

IN SAMARIA

After the stoning- death of Stephen, a follower of Jesus Christ, a great persecution broke out against the church in Jerusalem. All except the Apostles were scattered throughout Judea and Samaria. Those who had been scattered preached the word wherever they went, empowered and given boldness by the Holy Spirit.

Eight years after the Day of Pentecost, Philip one of Jesus followers, went down to Samaria and proclaimed the Gospel. Philip preached and also did many miraculous signs. As a result many people turned to Jesus Christ including a former sorcerer called Simon. *"But when they believed Philip as he preached the good news of the kingdom of God and the name of Jesus Christ, they were baptized, both men and women. Simon himself believed and was baptized"* – Acts 8:12.

When the apostles in Jerusalem heard that Samaria has accepted the word of God, they sent Peter and John to them. When Peter and John arrived, the first thing they wanted to find out was if these Believers were filled with the Spirit. From experience Peter knew only too well that he only became bold after he received the Holy Spirit on the Day of Pentecost. He knew that no amount of teaching would give them the power that they needed to live as Christians during this time of persecution. So what was the very first thing that they did before they taught them? *"When they arrived, they prayed for them that they may receive the Holy Spirit,* **because the Holy Spirit had not yet come upon any of them***; they had simply been baptized into the name of the Lord"* – Acts 8:15.

Here were people who were born-again and yet we are told that they had not yet received the Holy Spirit. This cancels the belief that many Christians have, that the Holy spirit comes upon Believers the same way that it did on the Day of Pentecost, when they become Christians. *"Then Peter and John placed their hands on them, and **they received the Holy Spirit***" – Acts 8:17. There are people who argue that the Bible does not say that they spoke in tongues as a sign that the Holy Spirit had come upon them. Let us look closely at what happened.

Simon the former sorcerer who had now become a Believer desired this ability to lay hands on people and they are immediately filled with the Holy Spirit, and he offered money to the apostles. *"When Simon **saw** that the Spirit was given at the laying on of the apostles' hands, he offered them money . . ."* – Acts 8:18. We cannot see the Spirit. What was it then that Simon saw that proved that the Spirit had come on an individual? – When hands were laid on them they started speaking in tongues. Today Christians are often afraid or embarrassed - or both – to ask a Believer whether they have been filled with the Holy Spirit. Not so in the early Church! It was so important to be filled with the Holy Spirit that this was the first question that the apostles asked new Believers in Jesus Christ. The unfortunate result is that we do not see the supernatural manifesting in most churches. People walk into and out of church Sunday after Sunday with the world not seeing what the difference is between them and the faithful who go to church! When the Church of Christ lets the Holy Spirit come upon them with power, the supernatural manifestations in their lives will draw people into the churches the same way that it drew people on the Day of Pentecost!

IN EPHESUS

About ten years after the Day of Pentecost Paul the apostle went to Ephesus on one of his missionary journeys. When he arrived there he found that apparently a Jew named Apollos had already gone to Ephesus before him, preached about Jesus and made some disciples. The Bible describes to us who Apollos was so that we can understand what kind of disciples Paul found in Ephesus. Jesus said, *"A student is not above his teacher, but everyone who is fully trained **will be like his teacher**"* – Luke 6:40. If we want to know about these disciples in Ephesus then we need to find out about Apollos who was their teacher (Acts 18:24-28).

We are told that Apollos was a learned man, with a thorough knowledge of the Scriptures. These disciples, like their teacher, probably had a thorough knowledge of the Scripture. Secondly we are told that Apollos had been instructed in the way of the Lord. He spoke with great fervour and taught about Jesus accurately, though he only knew about the baptism of John (water baptism). Apollos' disciples were taught about Jesus accurately. They understood who Jesus was and understood His mission on earth, and the fact that He was going to come back to take His people to heaven. However, they knew only one baptism – the baptism of John. We are told that Apollos spoke very boldly in the synagogue. While speaking there, a more mature Christian couple that had a church that met at their house (Romans 16:19) heard him speak, and realized that he needed to be grounded in the word a little bit more. *"When Priscilla and Aquila heard him, they invited him to their home and explained to him the way of God more adequately"* – Acts 18:26. Priscilla and Aquila probably taught Apollos about Jesus' baptism, which he did not know about. What was Jesus' baptism? John the Baptist is the one who first told people about Jesus' baptism. " . . . *The man on whom you see the Spirit come down and remain is he who will baptize with the Holy Spirit*" – John 1:33. There is no doubt that Apollos had zeal. However, it was zeal without full knowledge! Priscilla and Aquila had spent some time with Paul (Acts 18:18), and anyone who was around Paul, as we see when he meets the disciples in Ephesus, knew that he greatly emphasised being filled with the Holy Spirit!

When Paul found Apollos' disciples in Ephesus he watched them and saw that they were zealous and had a thorough knowledge of the Scriptures but that they lacked power and boldness! This must be the reason why he asked them, " . . .***Did you receive the Holy Spirit when you believed?***" Acts 19:2. Since these were Apollos' disciples and they only knew about John's baptism, their answer in the same verse is not surprising. "*No, we have not even heard that there is a Holy Spirit.*" Wow! They were disciples and yet they had not even heard that there was a Holy Spirit? Like we have mentioned, we will only know as much as our teacher knows!

When Paul asked them what baptism they had received, they said it was John's baptism. Paul went ahead to explain to them about John's baptism. " . . .*John's baptism was a baptism of repentance. He told the people to believe in the one coming after him, that is, Jesus*" – Acts 19:4. After Paul explained this to them, they were now ready for the baptism of Jesus. "*When Paul placed his hands on them, the Holy spirit came on them, and they spoke in tongues and prophesied.* **There were about twelve men in all**" – Acts 19:6-7. This passage about Apollos and his disciples show us that if we have only experienced the baptism of John, which is repentance and belief in the Lord Jesus Christ, then we need to have explained to us " . . .*the way of God more adequately*" – Acts 18:26.

Why are we told that there were twelve men in all? Without the power of the Holy Spirit, and only teaching through a thorough knowledge of the Scripture, Apollos only managed to make twelve disciples. On the Day of Pentecost when Peter preached under the power of the Holy Spirit, three thousand people were added to their number! - Acts 2:41. Soon after that, Peter and John healed a crippled beggar and after preaching to the crowd that had gathered another two thousand people were added to them. *"But many who heard the message believed, and the number of men grew to about five thousand"* – Acts 4:4. Supernatural power was what was leading these men! That power was received when the Holy Spirit came upon them!

9

The Gifts of the Holy Spirit

BUT TO EACH ONE OF US GRACE *has been given as Christ apportioned it. This is why it says: 'When he ascended on high, he led captives in his train and gave gifts to men' "* – Ephesians 4:8. This passage seems to claim that grace and gifts are one and the same. Since 'grace' is, undeserved favour, then we can see how it is connected to gifts. We often do not have to deserve a gift. A birthday present, for example, will be given to us because it is our birthday and not because we deserve it. A birthday present is therefore, grace.

This verse also claims that it has been given **to each one of us.**

No Believer in Jesus Christ can say that He has not given them a gift. The truth is that although everyone has been given a gift, these gifts do not manifest in everyone. There are people who walk fully in their gift and are a blessing to the Body of Christ. For others, though the gift is in there, unfortunately it is dormant. Paul exhorted us not to ignore spiritual gifts, but to seek to know about them. *"Now about spiritual gifts, brother, I do not want you to be ignorant"* – 1 Corinthians 12:1.

As we have seen in the previous chapter, the first thing that Paul enquired about when he met Believers was whether they have received the Holy Spirit. Paul did not separate salvation and the infilling of the Holy Spirit the way some churches have done today. To him, as soon as a person became a Christian, they needed to be filled with the Holy Spirit! That is why when Paul is talking to the Corinthians he can tell them, *"For we were **all** baptized by one Spirit into one body . . .and **we were all given the one Spirit to drink**"* – 1 Corinthians 12:13. Paul can safely say **all**, because he made sure that every Believer was filled with the Holy Spirit. However there is a new and interesting subject matter that Paul introduces here. When the Holy Spirit comes upon us, **we drink Him**!

LIVING WATER

Jesus talked a lot about water. One of the most memorable passages of Scripture about water is when He meets the woman at the well and asks her for water (John 4). When the Samaritan woman asked Him how He could ask her for a drink when Jews did not speak to Samaritans He tells her, *"It you knew **the gift of God** and who it is that asks you for a drink, you would have asked him and he* *would have given you **living water**"* – John 4:10. Who is Jesus talking about when He refers to "The gift of God"? He is referring to the Holy Spirit! The Holy Spirit is Living Water, and we drink of Him when He comes upon us, as Paul told the Corinthians – We were all given one Spirit to drink! This is also why Jesus said, *"If anyone is thirsty, let him come to me and drink. Whoever believes in me, as the Scripture has said,* **steams of living water will flow from within him**" – John 7:37. Jesus confused a lot of people through the words that He spoke. Many times He spoke in parables that the people did not understand. When Jesus talked of this living water, a lot of people may have wondered what He meant. The Amplified Version says, *"He who believes in Me (who cleaves to and trusts in and relies on Me) as the Scripture has said, from his innermost being shall flow (continuously) springs and rivers of living water."*

Although Jesus did not clarify further what this mysterious water was, thank God John clarifies for us what He meant. **"By this he meant the Spirit whom those who believed in him were later to receive.** *Up to that time the Spirit had not yet been given, since Jesus had not yet been glorified"* – John 7:39. Praise the Lord! If the Holy Spirit has come upon me then my belly is full of living water that needs to flow out and touch the people around me!

From where does the Holy Spirit get this living water? He gets it from heaven! *"For the Lamb at the centre of the throne will be their shepherd; '**he will lead them to springs of living water**.' "* – Revelation 7:17. The springs of living water are in heaven. When the Holy Spirit comes upon us, He fills our belly with water from the springs of living water that are in heaven. No wonder Jesus said of the Holy Spirit, *"He will bring glory to me* **by taking from what is mine and making it known to you**" – John 16:14. The springs of living water belong to God, but the Holy Spirit takes it and makes it know to us by giving it to us generously. Precious Holy Spirit, thank you! Jesus has identified Himself as the good Shepherd. He takes us to springs of living water when he baptizes us with the Holy Spirit. Only the Holy Spirit can quench our thirst! The book of Revelation talks about a new heaven in chapter 21. Seated on the throne is God Himself. Listen to what He says about this water. *"He who was seated on the throne said. 'I am making everything new!'* ... *'Write this down for these words are trustworthy and true.'* ... **'To him who is thirsty I will give to drink without cost from the spring of the water of life'** – Revelation 21:5-6. The Holy Spirit gives to all He comes upon, the water of life! Even the prophet Isaiah prophesied about this living water when he said, "**Come, all you who are thirsty, come to the waters; and you who have no money, come, buy and eat!**" – Isaiah 55:1. Praise God that the Holy Spirit is poured upon us free of charge!

Why do we drink from these springs of living water? - To water the gift(s) in us and cause it to manifest and grow. Water makes things grow. The apostle Paul told his disciple Timothy, not to neglect his spiritual gift, which was made known to him through a word of prophecy when a body of elders laid hands on him. We are going to take a look at the gifts that Christ has given His children. Although Timothy already had the gift, Paul his 'father' and mentor told him that the way of not ignoring his gift was by fanning it into a flame. *"For this reason I remind you to **fan into flame** the gift of God, which is in you through the laying on of my hands"* – 2 Timothy 1:6. How do we fan a gift that is there but not burning brightly? I believe that we do that through speaking in tongues!

WHAT ARE THESE GIFTS?

The first thing we must realize is that the gifts that we have received by grace, are not for our own selfish use, but are for the Body of Christ. *"Now to each one the manifestation of the Spirit is given for the common good . . .and he gives them to each one just as he determines"* – 1 Corinthians 12:7-11.

These gifts that have been bestowed on the children of God through His grace and mercy are recorded for us in two different books of the New Testament. The gifts that are identified in 1 Corinthians 12:8-10 are:

- The message of wisdom.
- The message of knowledge.
- Faith.
- Gifts of healing (People may have a gift for healing a particular ailment).
- Miraculous powers (there is a difference between a miracle and a healing).
- Prophecy.
- Distinguishing between spirits.
- Speaking in different kinds of tongues.
- The interpretation of tongues.

The gifts identified in Romans 12:6-8:

- Serving.
- Teaching.

- Encouraging.
- Contributing to the needs of others.
- Leadership.
- Showing mercy.

I believe that every Believer needs to know what his or her gift is so that they can us it to serve the Church of Christ. It is also good to notice that love, is not a gift! We have all been called to love as Christ has also loved us. Neither is finding the faults in others a gift!

What is our responsibility with the gifts that God has given us? We find the answer in the parable of the talents found in Matthew 25:14-30. In this parable, a man going on a journey gave talents of money to three workers, each according to his ability. The master did not discriminate. Each person got something. However, how much each got depended on his ability. To the first man he gave five talents, to the second he gave two and to the third man, he gave only one. When the master came back, the first and second man had doubled their talents through hard work. Although the first man now had ten talents while the second man had only four, they received the same praise from their master. *"His master replied, 'Well done good and faithful servant! You have been faithful with a few things' I will put you in charge of many things,* come and share your master's happiness"* – Matthew 25:21. The third man hid his talents in the ground, while complaining about how unfair his master was. The master gave each man the talents **according to their ability**. Even before the master gave the men the talents he already knew the ability of each man. It is you and I who did not know the ability of the three men. All that the master was looking for was **increase**. We can learn from this parable that when God gives us a particular gift,

He wants to see increase. I believe that the greatest enabler for the multiplying of gifts is the Holy Spirit! He empowers us to walk in our gift in increasing measure as we drink from His springs of living water! God in His wisdom knows who to give what gift, according to what He has called them to do here on earth.

There are people who confuse the gifts of the Spirit and the fruit of the Spirit. The difference is that the gifts are given to each individual as God determines while the **fruit of the Spirit** is given to everyone at salvation. When the Spirit is deposited in our spirit, He comes in with His fruit that is love, peace, patience, kindness, goodness, faithfulness, gentleness, and self-control. While the gifts manifest and increase supernaturally as we yield to the Holy Spirit, the fruit has to be **cultivated**. Work has to be put in for fruit to manifest. A good analogy of the difference between a gift and a fruit is a Christmas tree and a natural tree. While we simply put gifts under the Christmas tree, we have to water the natural tree and put it where it can receive sunshine if we want to see any fruit. Sometimes we have to add manure.

In 2 Peter 1:5 we are told to " . . . *Make every effort to add to your faith goodness; and to goodness, knowledge; and to knowledge. Self-control; and to self-control, perseverance; and to perseverance, godliness; and to godliness, brotherly kindness; and to brotherly kindness, love. For if you possess these qualities* **in increasing measure***, they will keep you from being ineffective and unproductive . . .*" However, when the Holy Spirit comes upon us, we are empowered to make the effort to add to these things mentioned above.

10

Speaking In Tongues

PRAYING IN TONGUES IS ONE OF THE MOST neglect weapons for spiritual warfare that the Bible tells us about. In Ephesians 6:17-18 we are encouraged to *"Take the helmet of salvation and the sword of the Spirit, which is the word of God. **And pray in the Spirit on all occasions.**"* Praying in tongues is a piece of armour with which we can defeat the devil in his schemes against us. We are exhorted to put on **the full armour of God** so that we can take our stand against the devil's schemes (Ephesians 6:11). When we do not have the gift of praying in the Spirit – through speaking in tongues – we do not have the full armour!

The only time when Satan does not understand what I am saying is when I am speaking (praying) in tongues! Since he does not know what God and I are planning together against him, he flees!

The apostle Paul told us in 1 Corinthians 14:2, that anyone who speaks in a tongue does not speak to men but to God. "*Indeed no one understand him (not even the devil); he utters mysteries with his spirit.*" Why would anyone speak to God in a language that they do not know? Let us explore why. When a person speaks to God, the assumption is that they want God to hear them. Otherwise their prayer would be futile. What makes God hear us? We find the answer in 1 John 5:14. "*This is the **confidence** we have in approaching God; that if we ask anything **according to his will** he hears us.*" The first point is that for God to hear us, we need to have confidence, and ask for whatever it is according to His will. Once He hears us then "*. . . We know that we have what we asked of him.*" When I walk away from prayer I should have confidence not only that God has heard me, but also that I have received what I asked of Him because I asked in His will.

How do I know God's will concerning a matter that I want to pray about? The fact is that as human beings we often do not know what God's will is concerning the issues that we pray about. I believe that is why many of our prayers receive "No" for an answer! We have a problem, and the problem is that we do not know what to pray for. Praise God that because He always wants to answer His children's prayers He has given us somebody to pray on our behalf. "*In the same way, **the Spirit helps us in our weakness. We do not know what we ought to pray for**, but the Spirit himself intercedes for us with groans that words cannot express*" – Romans 8:26. This is why the apostle Paul told the Corinthians, "I would like everyone of you to speak in tongues. . ." – 1 Corinthians 14:5.

The Holy Spirit is the only person who qualifies to pray in a way that God always answers. He knows the thoughts and will of God. *"But God has revealed it to us by his Spirit. The Spirit searches all things, even the deep things of God . . .**no one knows the thoughts of God except the Spirit of God***"* – 1 Corinthians 2:11. The Holy Spirit knows exactly what God is thinking, and His will, concerning any and every issue that I could ever want to pray for. No wonder we are exhorted to *" . . .Pray in the Spirit **on all occasions** with all kinds of prayers and requests . . ."* – Ephesians 6:18. All occasions means – Every time! Although we should pray in the Spirit every time we pray Paul says that we should not only pray in tongues all the time. Why is this? *"For if I pray in a tongue, my spirit prays, **but my mind is unfruitful**"* – 1 Corinthians 14:14. What does Paul say we should do to solve this problem? *"So what shall I do? I will pray with my spirit, **but I will also** pray with my mind. I will sing with my spirit, but **I will also** sing with my mind"* – 1 Corinthians 14:13-14. The implication is that we should always pray in tongues **and also pray with our minds.** Many people have turned it the other way round – They pray with their minds, **and also with their spirit.** In this verse, praying in the Spirit is given first priority. Why is that? When I start off by praying in the Spirit, the spirit renews my mind so that when I pray with a renewed mind, I pray the will and thoughts of God! If I start off praying with my mind, I am starting from a position of not knowing what God's will is and I will not have confidence. Hebrews 4:16, tells us to approach the throne of God with confidence. We already saw in 1 John 5:14 that the confidence that we have is from knowing that we are praying in the will of God. So if I am to approach the throne of God with confidence then that means that I approach the throne of God praying in tongues!

We can see then, that praying in tongues is not an option for a select few. We are told that he who speaks in a tongue edifies himself – 1 Corinthians 14:4. To edify means to strengthen or build up. The original meaning in Latin means, "construct a building." Which Christian does not want to be built up in their faith? *"But you dear friends **build yourselves up** in your most holy faith and pray in the Holy Spirit"* – Jude 20. We have also been told that whoever speaks in a tongue speaks to God. Which Christian does not need to talk to God?

Important as speaking in tongues is, Paul tells us that tongues must be spoken within a context, and that context is love. *"If I speak in tongues of men and of angels, **but have not love**, I am only a resounding gong or a clanging cymbal"* – 1 Corinthians 13:1. One Bible commentator has said that 1 Corinthians 13 was placed between the two chapters on the gifts of the Spirit for a reason. Love is what is inside this "sandwich." As Paul begins chapter 14, he says, *"**Follow the way of love . . .**"*

Thankfully, love is a fruit of the Holy Spirit. When I speak in tongues I water what is within me and cause it to manifest. I believe what Paul is saying here is that when we see somebody who is not walking in love praying in tongues, then we have to questions whether those tongues are really from the Holy Spirit! God is love, and if God and the Holy Spirit are one, then the Holy Spirit is also love!

ARE TONGUES FOR EVERYONE?

Although it should be obvious to everyone by now that tongues are for all believers, there are a few verses in the Bible that have confused some people, making them believe that tongues are not for everyone. In 1 Corinthians 12:28-31 Paul, teaching on the subject of gifts mentions that God has appointed in the church first of all apostles, second prophets and third teachers. Then he goes on to enumerate the gifts: workers of miracles, those having gifts of healing (notice that he does not say '**the gift** of healing'. People have a gift to heal different things within the body), those able to help others, those with gifts of administration (again he does not say 'the gift of administration' but gifts in different aspects of administration), speaking in different kinds of tongues.

Then Paul goes on to ask rhetorical questions. Are all apostles? Are all prophets? Are all teachers? Do all work miracles? Do all have gifts of heal? **Do all speak in tongues**? Do all interpret? When a lot of people get to this verse they often say, "Aha! It says here that all do not speak in tongues." They are actually right! The gift of speaking in different kinds of **tongues** (1 Corinthians 12:10), is only for a select few. However, speaking in **a tongue**, to God and not to men, is for everybody! You will notice that each time the gift for the church is mentioned, it is in plural. The tongue for the individual is in a singular tense.

- *"For anyone who speaks in **a tongue**, does not speak to men but to God. No one understands him; he utters mysteries with his spirit"* - 1 Corinthians 14:2.

- *"He who speaks in **a tongue** edifies himself..."* - 1 Corinthians 14:4

These two verses show us that the private prayer to God is in **a tongue**. This is a person praying alone in their room or only loud enough for God and himself to hear, in a meeting of Believers.

Nobody needs to know what he or she is saying because they are talking to God and not to men. They are strengthening and encouraging **themselves**, and not the church. **This gift of praying in a tongue is for all Believers**. It is their secret weapon against Satan who does not understand what they are saying to God.

Concerning praying in different kinds of tongues, a gift for the church, Paul says:

- "... *He who prophesies is greater than he who speaks in tongues, unless he interprets,* **so that the church may be edified**" – 1 Corinthians 14:5.
- "I thank God that I speak **in tongues** more than all of you. But **in the church** I would rather speak five intelligible words to instruct others than ten thousand words in **a tongue**" – 1 Corinthians 14:18-19.

Notice that Paul does not say ten thousand words in tongues, but in a tongue.

The context of these two latter verses is the church. This is somebody who is at a church meeting and then speaks to the Believers in tongues. Paul says that within the context of a church meeting, there must always be an interpretation of the tongues otherwise "*If there is no interpreter, the speaker should keep quiet in the church* **and speak to himself (in a tongue) and God**" – 1 Corinthians 14:28. Paul does not say keep quiet and do not speak, but only speak to God, and not to the church – and there is a big difference!

I have been to churches where somebody will speak in tongues in a loud voice for everybody to hear and then an interpretation does not follow. That ought not to be. Paul says that if people speak in tongues in a church meeting, " . . .*Two or at the most three should speak, one at a time, **and someone must interpret*** " – 1 Corinthians 14:27. Why is this? *"For God is not a God of disorder but of peace . . ."* – 1 Corinthians 14:33.

Conclusion

Jesus kept His promise of sending us another Counsellor to be with us and in us. He is the Holy Spirit who came down on the Day of Pentecost, transforming weak fearful men into the giants of faith that we read about in the Bible today!

This great and marvellous Counsellor has come to teach us all things. He is called the Spirit of truth. He is our Encourager and Comforter - A friend that sticks closer than a brother! Since He knows the thoughts and the will of God, He is able to get our payers answered when we pray through Him.

Have you received the Holy Spirit or like the disciples in Ephesus you only know the baptism of John? John himself said that the One who was coming after him was greater than him. John said that he baptised with water, but Jesus would baptise with the Holy Spirit and with fire! This baptism is available for every Believer – even YOU! Do not hold back anymore. If you have not yet been baptised in the Holy Spirit then today is your day. All you need to do is ask *"If you then, though you are evil, know how to give good gifts to your children,* **how much more will your father in heaven give the Holy Spirit to those who ask him***!"*

Once you have asked, just simply receive Him and say "Thank you Lord for the Holy Spirit. I receive Him right now in the name of Jesus Christ!" Spend some time just worshiping God and thanking Him for all that He has done in your life. Then open your mouth and start to praise him in a heavenly language that you have not known before. When you start the devil will tell you that you are making up the words. Just ignore him and by faith continue speaking in the new language. If the Holy Spirit gives you just two words, then repeat those two words over and over until He gives you more vocabulary. Like all languages, the more you pray in your new language the more words will be added to you. Your tongue will build up more and more each day! Continue to thank the Lord for this wonderful gift! Tell somebody close to you what God has done for you so they can also rejoice with you. If they do not speak in tongues then give them this book to read and encourage them to receive this wonderful gift!

May be you do not know Jesus Christ as your personal Saviour. This is the time to give your life to your wonderful Saviour who died on the cross for your sins. You do not have to continue living a life of struggle, leading your own life and messing up each tine you try to live right. Your struggle is over. Find a quiet place where you can talk alone to God and say the prayer below.

SAMPLE PRAYER

Just say these simple words and mean them from the bottom of your heart . . .

O Lord God, I believe in Jesus Christ the Son of the Living God. I believe He died for me and You raised Him from the dead. Right now I confess with my mouth, Jesus Christ is Lord of my life. From this day, I thank you Lord for saving my soul. I have eternal life now - In the name of the Lord Jesus Christ. Thank you Lord! I am a child of God from this day forward – Amen! Praise the Lord!

If you have prayed this prayer and meant it from the bottom of your heart, then you are now a child of God! Welcome to the kingdom of God! The Bible tells us that all the angels in heaven rejoice when one sinner comes to Jesus Christ! Please find a Christian and tell them of this very important decision that you have made. Find a Bible- believing church where you can fellowship with other believers. Go up to the pastor and tell him that you have recently made a decision to follow Jesus Christ. If possible, join a small Bible study group where you can learn how to conduct your life according to the word of God. Remember that if a baby is born and not taken care of, he or she will die! Babies need milk, which is like the word of God for the believer. There are many devotional books that you can find from a Christian bookstore. Use it to guide you as you read the Bible. God bless you!

About The Author

Pastor Nellie Shani, who has been a Christian for over three decades, is founder and CEO of Breaking Barriers International (BBI), a non-profit organization whose mission is to equip believers in Jesus Christ to live victoriously and fulfil their purpose in the world. Nellie has adhered to this mission through her regular teachings on spiritual warfare and deliverance. Her profound revelation of the word of God is taught with clarity and simplicity. As conference speaker and workshop leader, Pastor Nellie has been used by God to teach and train believers in the area of spiritual warfare in Africa, the United States of America, the United Kingdom, and Eastern Europe.

As a happily married woman she has three grown children and one son-in-law. She draws her knowledge and experience from having lived with her family in six different countries, on three continents.

OTHER BOOKS BY AUTHOR

STAND YOUR GROUND
Many Christians live a life of defeat, harassed and bombarded by their archenemy, Satan. They have not yet fully grasped that when Jesus Christ died on the cross, he completely and utterly defeated Satan! He took back the authority Satan used to deceive Adam and Eve, handing it to the Church. However, our strength is of no use if we don't know we possess it! This is the tragedy of our Lack of Knowledge.

BREAKING INVISIBLE BARRIERS
Many Christians today are living a life of constant struggle and failure no matter what they do to try and improve their lot in life. They are fighting something they do not understand. This book explores these invisible barriers and how to break them by the Power of the Cross.

HOPE FOR THE CHILDLESS
God designed that every womb He has created be fruitful. Why then do we have people who cannot have children? This book answers this question and shares the experiences of women who were not able to conceive or carry babies to full term, but today are mothers by the grace of God.

WHEN TWO HALVES MAKE A HOLE…
Battling for Our Marriages
Behind every broken marriage is a fierce battle that was lost in the spiritual realm. Many people do not realize that from the moment that they say, "I do" a raging battle starts whose sole objective is the break-up of the marriage. The Bible warns us that our enemy the devil prowls around like a roaring lion looking for someone to devour. We are told not to be a passive onlooker but to "Resist him…" Thus battling for our marriage is not an option but a command.

UNGODLY SOUL TIES
Did you know that there are relationships that we walked away from as many as ten years ago that can still keep us in bondage? Many people are not aware that the way they behave today may be directly related to the way their parents, or even a kindergarten teacher treated them in childhood. Ungodly soul ties are often forged between us, and people who have abused us physically, emotionally or psychologically. This book will tell you how to identify and break them through the power of the cross of Jesus Christ.

www.ingramcontent.com/pod-product-compliance
Lightning Source LLC
LaVergne TN
LVHW051848080426
835512LV00018B/3136